This Book belongs to:

Your Name

For Free Educational Posters:
Please Email: info@Kukendo.com

Created by:

- Kim Van Schoor (B.Admin): Mother of 3
- Claire Gill (B.Ed): Teacher 10 years
- Dr. Wendy Rawlinson (Ph.D. Education, Masters Linguistics): Grandmother of 6, Mother of 3

Supports the 5 crucial areas of childhood development

Educational fun, designed by teachers & Moms

2% profits donated to Children's education in Africa

Printed locally to reduce transport emissions

Thank You for supporting products with purpose:

2% of profits go towards children education in South Africa.

Together we are creating a brighter future for children around the world!

KUKENDO.COM

Your Adventure Starts Here!

Spring has arrived, nature is flourishing and excitement is in the air!
But every animal has come out to play at the same time!
Can you help find all the animals to check that they are safe?

INSTRUCTIONS

Step 1: Choose from 5x different Journeys below.
Step 2: There are 16 Landscapes. In each Landscape, Find the Animals & Objects for Your Chosen Journey
Step 3: Once You've Finished Each Landscape, Put a Tick on the Star Scoreboard Below:

Star Scoreboard

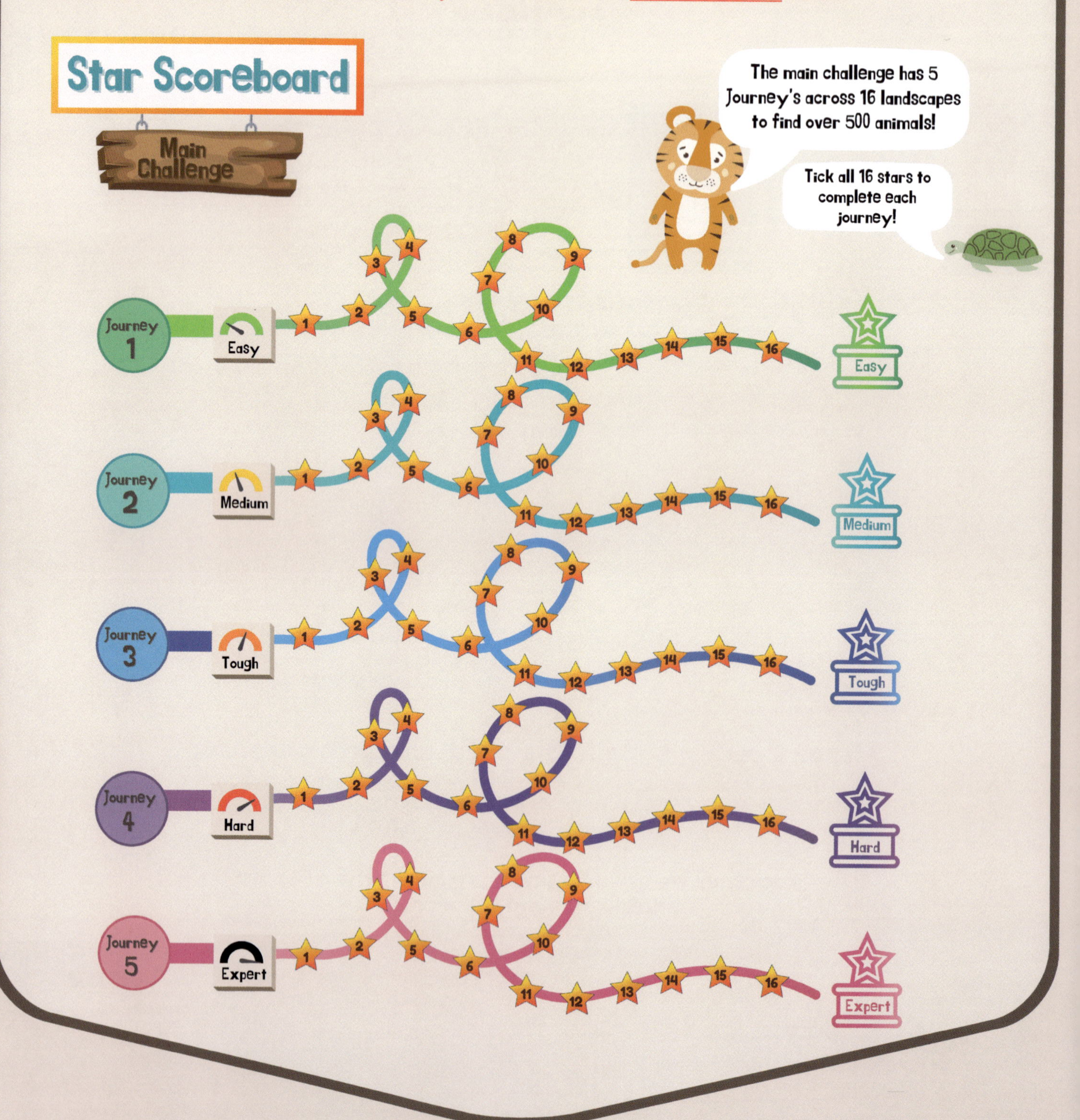

Extra Adventures Here...

There's an extra 1036 items to find in the book!

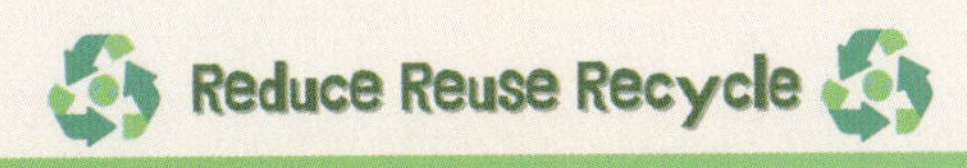

Recycle Rally

Challenge 2

Can You Find the Items for Recycling? Can You Choose the Correct Bin for each Item?

Oh no! It looks like people have left rubbish that doesn't belong in nature. Pollution is bad for the environment!

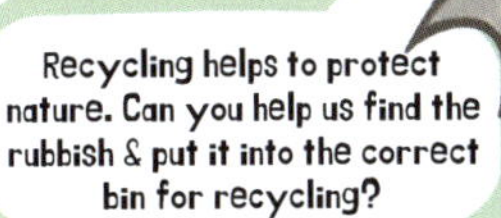

Recycling helps to protect nature. Can you help us find the rubbish & put it into the correct bin for recycling?

Tiny Balloon Bloom

Challenge 3

The tiny insect-balloon race is on! But this year the wind is strong & some balloons blew away. But we don't know which balloons!

Let's check which tiny balloons have blown away so we can make sure our friends are safe!

Can You Find every Balloon? In each Landscape: which Balloons are Missing?

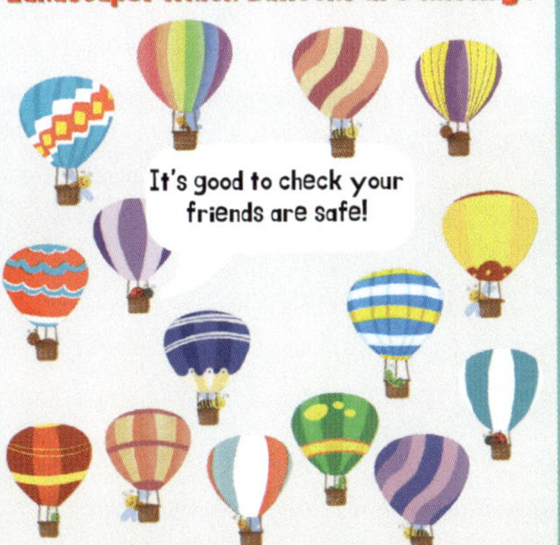

It's good to check your friends are safe!

Lost & Found

Challenge 4

I can't find my favorite jacket anywhere? I must have left it lying around.

I can't find my bike, I'm already sad that I lost it. It's important that we look after our things.

Let's go find our lost items. From now on we will always remember to keep our things safe!

Can You Help Find all the Valuable Lost-Items?

Mushroom Medley

Challenge 5

Each butterfly has lost their favorite mushroom to rest on. Can you help them?

Find each Butterfly & then Help Them Find Their Favorite Mushroom.

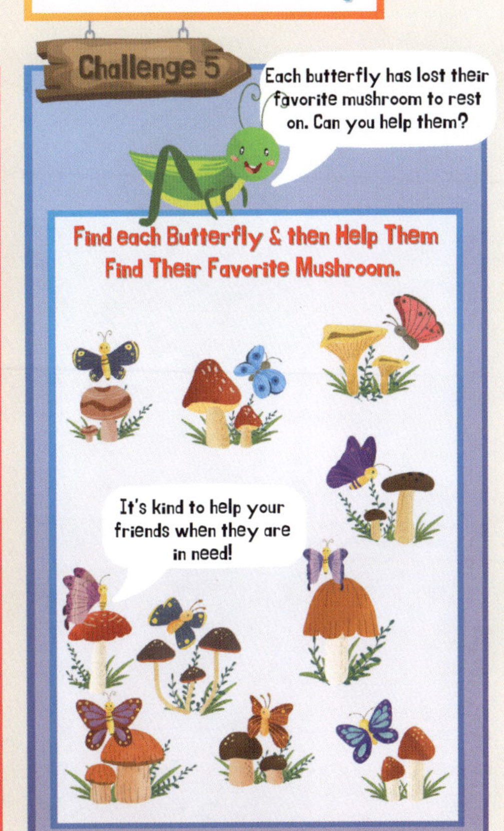

It's kind to help your friends when they are in need!

Bird Bonanza

Challenge 6

Fredrika Flamingo has a special talent, she remembers where each bird stays!

There is mayhem in the skies! All the birds are lost & trying to get home

I also need help: lets work together to find each bird. Then I can help guide them home!

Can You Find each bird so that Fredrika Flamingo can guide them home?

When you have a special talent, you can use it to help others!

Ask for help when you need & work together when you can!

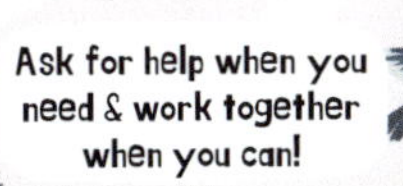

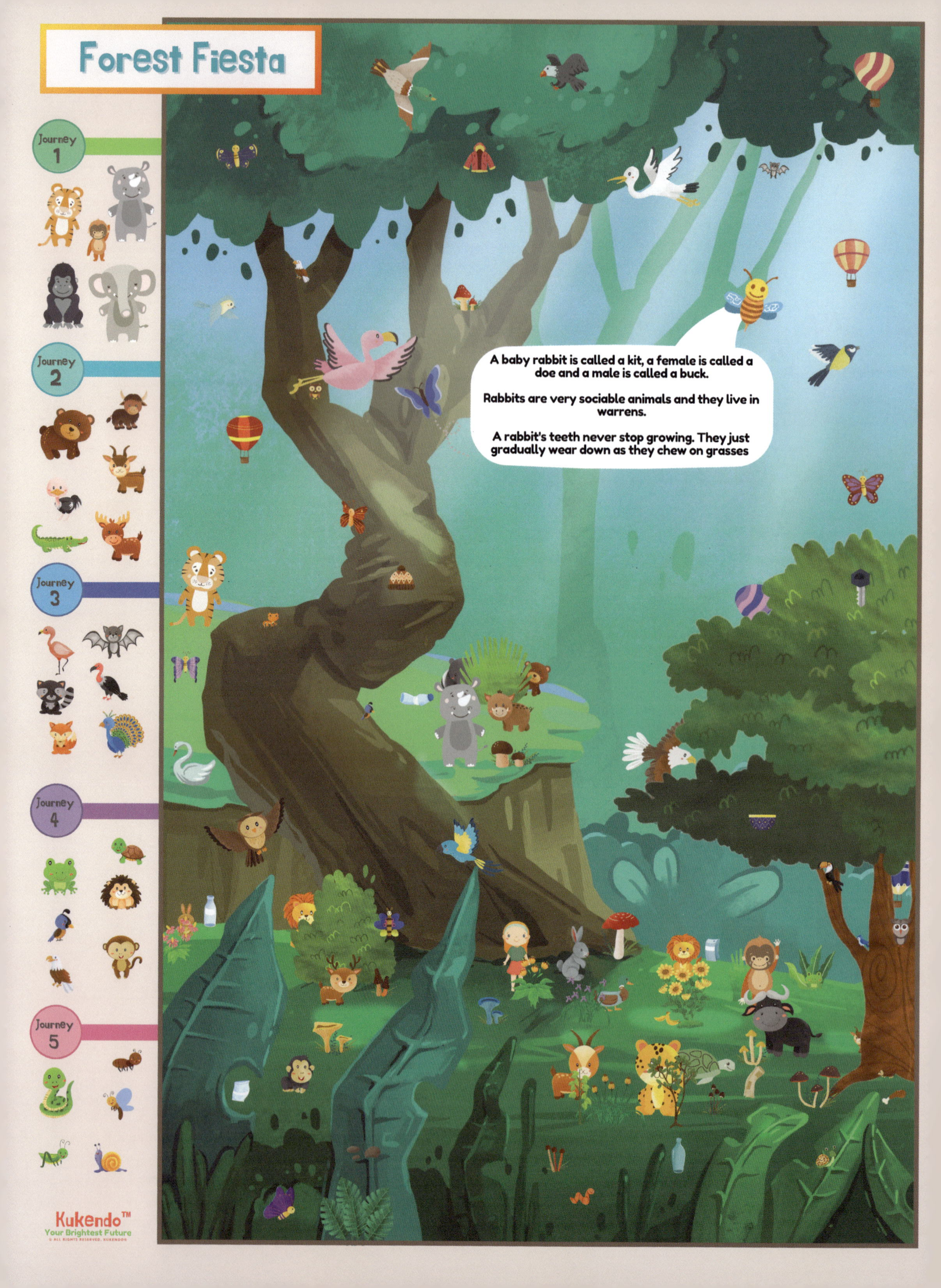
Forest Fiesta
Journey 1
Journey 2
Journey 3
Journey 4
Journey 5
A baby rabbit is called a kit, a female is called a doe and a male is called a buck.
Rabbits are very sociable animals and they live in warrens.
A rabbit's teeth never stop growing. They just gradually wear down as they chew on grasses
Kukendo™
Your Brightest Future

Extra Challenges
Organic
Paper
Glass
Metal
Plastic
Kukendo™
Play. Imagine. Learn
© ALL RIGHTS RESERVED. KUKENDO®

Sunken Shipwreck
Journey 1
Journey 2
Journey 3
Journey 4
Journey 5
Us sharks are the only fish that can blink.
There are over 30,000 species of fish that exist.
Did you know, fish can also get sunburn, just similar to humans!
Kukendo™
Your Brightest Future

Extra Challenges
Organic
Paper
Glass
Metal
Plastic
Kukendo™
Play. Imagine. Learn

Adventure Woods
Journey 1
Journey 2
Journey 3
Journey 4
Journey 5
A group of owls is called a Parliament
Owls can turn their heads as much as 270 degrees.
Aside from hooting, owls make a variety of calls, from whinnies to whistles to squeaks.
Kukendo™
Your Brightest Future

Extra Challenges
Organic
Paper
Glass
Metal
Plastic
Kukendo™
Play. Imagine. Learn

Rocky Path
A group of penguins in the water is called a raft but on land, they're called a waddle.
Many male penguins gift female penguins with rocks in order to woo them.
The black and white "tuxedo" look donned by most penguin species is a clever camouflage called countershading.
Journey 1
Journey 2
Journey 3
Journey 4
Journey 5
Kukendo™
Your Brightest Future

Extra Challenges
Organic
Paper
Glass
Metal
Plastic
Kukendo™
Play. Imagine. Learn
© ALL RIGHTS RESERVED. KUKENDO®

Coral Shores
Journey 1
Journey 2
Journey 3
Journey 4
Journey 5
An octopus has three hearts.
They have blue blood.
Octopus arms have a mind of their own. Two-thirds of an octopus' neurons reside in its arms, not its head.
Kukendo™
Your Brightest Future

Extra Challenges
Organic
Paper
Glass
Metal
Plastic

Spring Garden
Journey 1
Journey 2
Journey 3
Journey 4
Journey 5
There are about 10,000 bird species on the planet.
Instead of teeth, birds have gizzard that grinds up their food.
Around 4,000 bird species migrate to other countries.
Kukendo™
Your Brightest Future

Extra Challenges
Organic
Paper
Glass
Metal
Plastic

Secret Footpath
Journey 1
Journey 2
Journey 3
Journey 4
Journey 5
The wings of a butterfly are transparent.
While humans use tongues for taste, butterflies use their feet instead.
There are around 20,000 species of butterflies on Earth.
Kukendo™
Your Brightest Future

Extra Challenges
Organic
Paper
Glass
Metal
Plastic
Kukendo™
Play. Imagine. Learn
© ALL RIGHTS RESERVED. KUKENDO®

Paradise Waterfall
Journey 1
Journey 2
Journey 3
Journey 4
Journey 5
Ducks have 3 eyelids.
Ducks have no nerves or blood vessels in their feet. With that, their feet cannot feel hot or cold.
Ducks are found on every continent except Antarctica.
Kukendo™
Your Brightest Future

Extra Challenges
Organic
Paper
Glass
Metal
Plastic

Jungle Fun
Journey 1
Journey 2
Journey 3
Journey 4
Journey 5
In the US, almost 60% of all freshly cut flowers are grown in California.
Lilies are beautiful flowers, but they are highly toxic for cats.
The agave is known as a monocarpic plant, meaning it can stay dormant for years and only blooms once and then dies.
Kukendo™
Your Brightest Future

Extra Challenges
Organic
Paper
Glass
Metal
Plastic

Hot Savannah
Journey 1
Journey 2
Journey 3
Journey 4
Journey 5
Kukendo™
Your Brightest Future

Extra Challenges
Organic
Paper
Glass
Metal
Plastic
Missing Balloons
Giraffes only need to drink once every few days. Most of their water comes from all the plants they eat.
Giraffes spend most of their lives standing up; they even sleep and give birth standing up.
A giraffe's spots are much like human fingerprints. No two individual giraffes have exactly the same pattern.
Kukendo™
Play. Imagine. Learn
© ALL RIGHTS RESERVED. KUKENDO®

Deep Gully
Many jellyfish have bioluminescent organs which emit blue or green light, thus they glow in the dark.
Jellyfish don't have brains. Not only that, they also have no blood, no bones, and no heart, since they are made of 95% water.
c. Jellyfish have survived five mass extinctions, including the Great Dying (or the Permian-Triassic extinction event) which wiped out up to 70% of life on Earth.
Journey 1
Journey 2
Journey 3
Journey 4
Journey 5
Kukendo™
Your Brightest Future

Extra Challenges
Organic
Paper
Glass
Metal
Plastic

Peaceful Lake
Worms will become paralyzed if exposed to sunlight for a long time.
Worms can regenerate some segments of their body.
They can breathe through the skin since they don't have lungs.
Journey 1
Journey 2
Journey 3
Journey 4
Journey 5
Kukendo™
Your Brightest Future

Extra Challenges
Organic
Paper
Glass
Metal
Plastic
Kukendo™
Play. Imagine. Learn

Island Reef
Journey 1
Journey 2
Journey 3
Journey 4
Journey 5
Turtles have a second shell. Besides their outer shell, turtles also have a lower shell, called a plastron. The plastron usually joins with the upper shell—called the carapace—along both sides of the body to create a complete skeletal box.
Turtles lose their first "baby tooth" within an hour. Baby turtles, called hatchlings, have an "egg tooth" on their beak to help them hatch out of their shell. This tooth disappears approximately an hour after hatching.
Kukendo™
Your Brightest Future

Extra Challenges
Organic
Paper
Glass
Metal
Plastic
Kukendo™
Play. Imagine. Learn

Countryside Clearing
Journey 1
Journey 2
Journey 3
Journey 4
Journey 5
A group of penguins in the water is called a raft but on land they're called a waddle.
Many male penguins gift female penguins with rocks in order to woo them.
The black and white "tuxedo" look donned by most penguin species is a clever camouflage called countershading.
Kukendo™
Your Brightest Future

Extra Challenges
Organic
Paper
Glass
Metal
Plastic
Kukendo™
Play. Imagine. Learn
© ALL RIGHTS RESERVED. KUKENDO®

Mystery Canyon
The oldest known fossil of an insect dates back 400 million years.
There are about 91,000 species of insects in the United States.
To survive the cold of winter months, many insects replace their body water with a chemical called glycerol, which acts as an "antifreeze" against the temperatures.
Journey 1
Journey 2
Journey 3
Journey 4
Journey 5
Kukendo™
Your Brightest Future

Extra Challenges
Organic
Paper
Glass
Metal
Plastic
Missing Balloons
Kukendo™
Play. Imagine. Learn
© ALL RIGHTS RESERVED. KUKENDO®

Giant Woodland
Journey 1
Journey 2
Journey 3
Journey 4
Journey 5
Rabbits also purr just like cats.
Mother rabbits are pregnant for just about 28-31 days and can deliver 14 babies called kittens.
Rabbits can turn their ears by 180 degrees.
Kukendo™
Your Brightest Future

Extra Challenges
Organic
Paper
Glass
Metal
Plastic
Kukendo™
Play. Imagine. Learn
© ALL RIGHTS RESERVED, KUKENDO®

ANSWERS

For Large Answer Sheets (Free PDF download)
Please Email: info@Kukendo.com

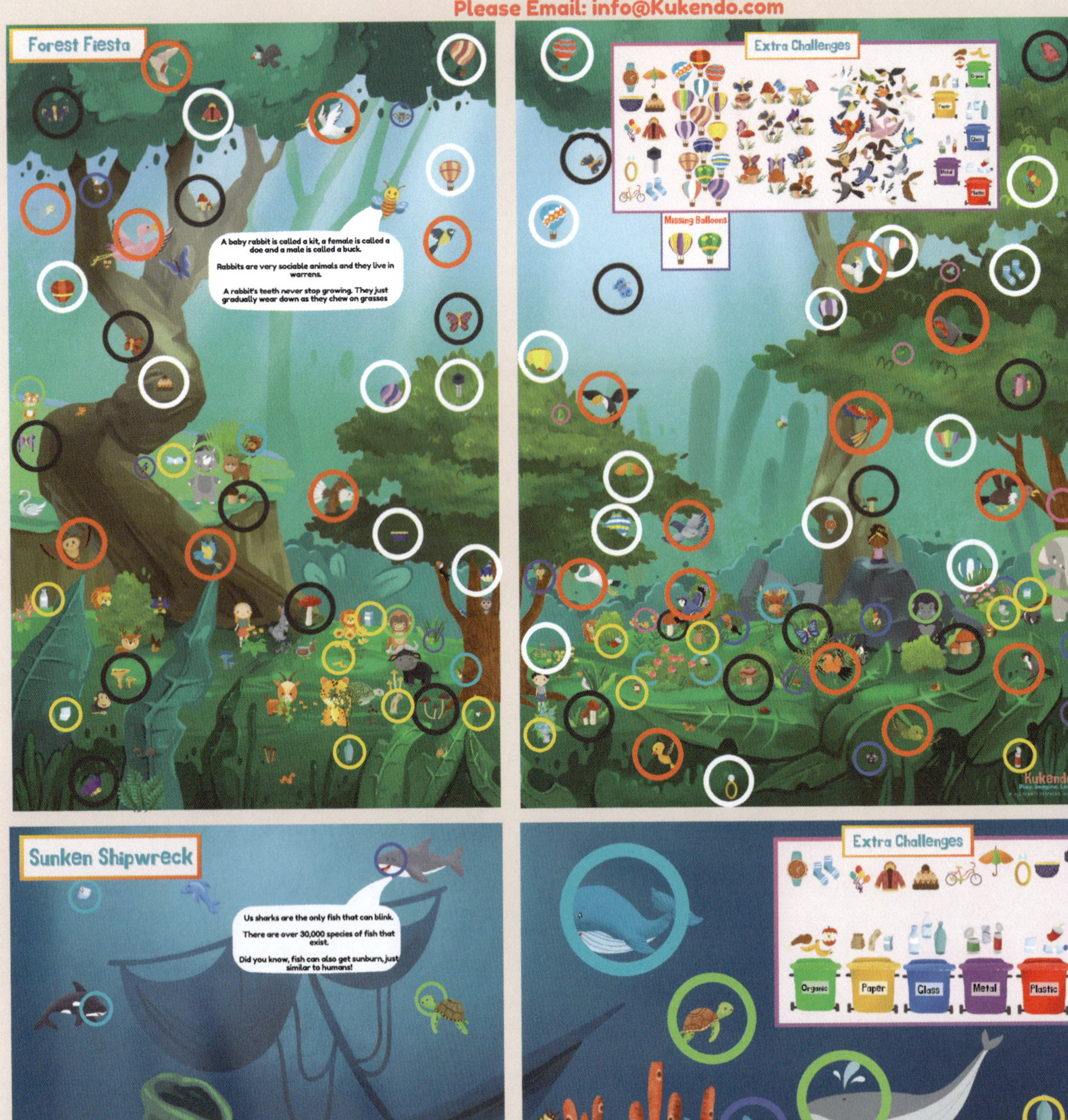

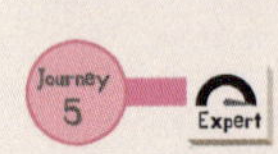

ANSWERS

For Large Answer Sheets (Free PDF download)
Please Email: info@Kukendo.com

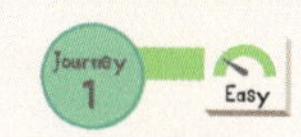

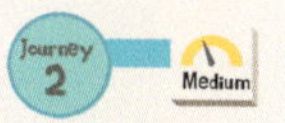

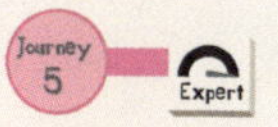

ANSWERS

For Large Answer Sheets (Free PDF download)
Please Email: info@Kukendo.com

Journey 1 — Easy

Journey 2 — Medium

Journey 3 — Tough

Journey 4 — Hard

Journey 5 — Expert

ANSWERS

For Large Answer Sheets (Free PDF download)
Please Email: info@Kukendo.com

Journey 1 Easy

Journey 2 Medium

Journey 3 Tough

Journey 4 Hard

Journey 5 Expert

ANSWERS

For Large Answer Sheets (Free PDF download)
Please Email: info@Kukendo.com

Journey 1 — Easy
Journey 2 — Medium
Journey 3 — Tough
Journey 4 — Hard
Journey 5 — Expert

ANSWERS

For Large Answer Sheets (Free PDF download)
Please Email: info@Kukendo.com

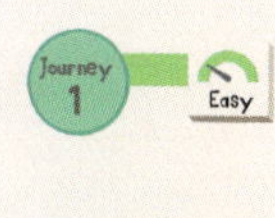

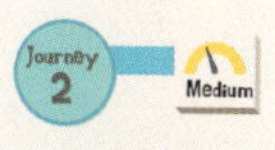

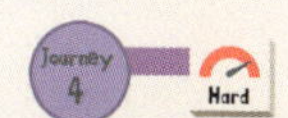

ANSWERS

For Large Answer Sheets (Free PDF download)
Please Email: info@Kukendo.com

Journey 1 — Easy

Journey 2 — Medium

Journey 3 — Tough

Journey 4 — Hard

Journey 5 — Expert

ANSWERS

For Large Answer Sheets (Free PDF download)
Please Email: info@Kukendo.com

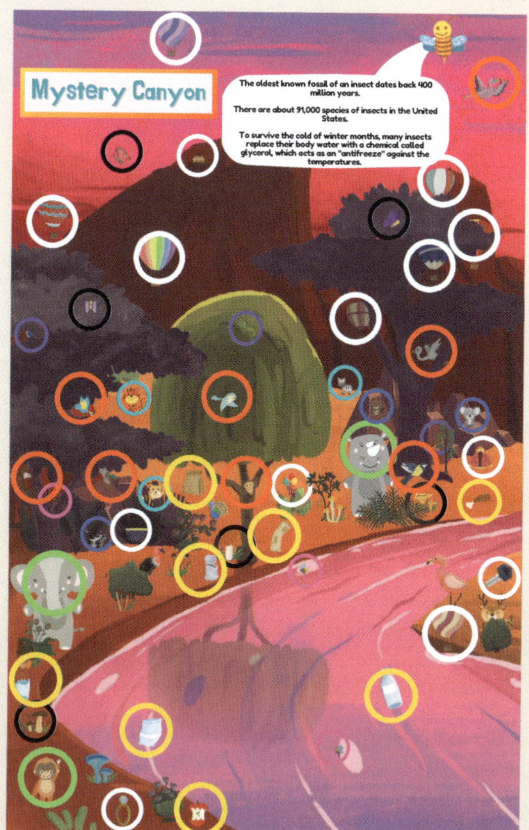

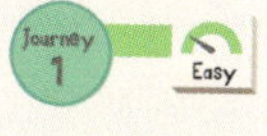

Our Story

KUKENDO MEANS "LOVE GROWING".

Our family brand started in the beautiful 'cradle of humankind': Africa (where we live & work).

One day we panicked..

As parents-to-be, we spent hours searching "how to be good parents"

- we realized:
your childhood really does impact the rest of your life.

So we set out to help our children:
We didn't have resources/money but we would do anything to give our kids what they need, for a happy and successful future.

The journey brought together many contributors who shared our passion: parents, teachers & a retired English professor. Together we discovered a simple truth to support each child's unique journey:

Make learning fun.

When you enjoy learning - you will keep developing into the best version of yourself, for the rest of your life. A lifetime of benefit.

Things aren't always easy in Africa, but the power of education allows our kids to rise up through any challenges. Skills quite literally change your future for the better. We are privileged to share these tools & resources with your family too.

Thanks to you, we can give back 2% of profits to help childhood education, giving kids the gift of education.

Welcome to the Kukendo Family,
May you & your family have the brightest future!

Printed in Great Britain
by Amazon